WOMEN
IN HISTORY

WOMEN AND BUSINESS

Miriam Moss

Wayland

F

WOMEN
IN HISTORY

Women and the Arts
Women and Business
Women and Education
Women and the Family
Women and Literature
Women and Politics
Women and Science
Women and Sport
Women and War
Women and Work

Series editor: Catherine Ellis
Consultant: Professor Deirdre Beddoe BA, PhD, Dip Ed, Reader in History at the Polytechnic of Wales
Designer: Joyce Chester

Front cover: *The Pork Butcher* by Camille Pissarro, 1883.
Back cover: Top left – A nineteenth-century greengrocer. Top right – Mary Quant, business woman and fashion designer poses with two of her outfits for her 1972 Autumn Collection. Bottom left – Anita Roddick, founder and managing director of The Body Shop International, in front of some of her products. Bottom right – painting of an eighteenth-century shopkeeper from Glasgow.

First published in 1990 by
Wayland (Publishers) Limited
61 Western Road, Hove
East Sussex BN3 1JD, England

© Copyright 1990 Wayland (Publishers) Limited

British Library Cataloguing in Publication Data
Moss, Miriam
    Women and business. – (Women in History)
    1. Women. Employment – Sociological perspectives
    I. Title   II. Series
    305.4'3

ISBN 1–85210–500–3

Typeset by Kalligraphics Limited, Horley, Surrey
Printed in Italy by G. Canale & C.S.p.A., and bound by MacLehose & Partners Limited, Portsmouth

Picture acknowledgements
The pictures in this book were supplied by the following: The Billie Love Collection 6, 7, 9, 15; The Bridgeman Art Library (front cover); Brighton Borough Council 43; Camera Press 32, 34, 37; Equal Opportunities Commission 41; FI Group Plc 36; Format Photographers 35; The Hulton Picture Library 10, 12, 13 (top), 14; Imperial War Museum 24; The Industrial Society 30; Institute of Directors 4, 40; London Enterprise Agency/Livewire 44; Mary Evans Picture Library back cover top left , 8, 11, 13 (bottom), 17, 18, 19, 20, (top and bottom), 21; Milgate Publishing Ltd 39; Munro & Forster PR back cover bottom left; The People's Palace (Glasgow Museums and Art Galleries) back cover bottom right, 7; Popperfoto back cover top right, 25, 26 (top and bottom), 27, 28, 29; Topham Picture Library 8, 42; Wayland Picture Library 5, 16, 23, 31; Women into Business 37 (top). The artwork on pages 31, 34, 37 was supplied by Malcolm Walker.

Permissions
The publisher would like to thank the following for allowing certain extracts to be used in the book: Controller of Her Majesty's Stationery Office for *Study of Female Business Owners, Department of Employment Research Paper 65*; Tavistock Publications for *In A Man's World* by Spencer and Podmore; Extract taken from *Family Fortunes* by L. Davidoff & C. Hall, reproduced by kind permission of Unwin Hyman Ltd; Weidenfeld & Nicolson for *Pile It High and Sell It Cheap* by Maurice Corina.

21115093M

TS

Contents

1 INTRODUCTION
page 4

2 EARLY BUSINESS WOMEN
page 5

3 INVISIBLE ASSETS 1780–1850
page 8

4 THE VICTORIAN ERA 1837–1901
page 13

5 NEW BUSINESS FOR WOMEN 1900–1945
page 20

6 THE POST-WAR YEARS 1945–1969
page 26

7 FEMALE ENTREPRENEURS 1970–1990
page 31

8 ENCOURAGING WOMEN INTO BUSINESS
page 37

9 THE WAY AHEAD
page 43

Projects – *page 45*
Books to Read – *page 46*
Glossary – *page 47*
Index – *page 48*

1

Introduction

Four of the finalists for the 1986 Veuve Clicquot Business Women of the Year Award – an award set up to help encourage business women.

‘

Ann Jaquin who was entered on the Freedom Roll of the Goldsmiths' company in 1746 took Elizabeth Bence as an apprentice:
Memorandum, That I Elizabeth Bence, Daur. of Peter Bence, late of the Parish of St. James, Westmr, in the County of Middlesex Chocolate Maker deced. Do put myself Apprentice to Ann Jaquin. Citizen and Goldsmith of London for the term of Seven Years from this Day there being paid to my said Mistress Thirty Pounds.   Elizabeth Bence.
Goldsmiths' Company Apprenticeship Book, 1747.

’

Women's business experience goes back hundreds of years, but their involvement in the world of business has been very different from men's. Many factors have influenced the ways in which women have been able to take part in business – changes in the birth-rate, the economy, education, effects of war and social pressures. This book provides an illustration of how women have participated in the economic activity of Britain. It deals particularly with the nineteenth and twentieth centuries, but it also looks back further to see how women's contribution to business has changed over the centuries.

The earliest form of business was simply an exchange of goods between one person and another. Today the word *business* covers a wide variety of activities, from selling hand-knitted jumpers in Covent Garden Market to the computerized business transactions involving millions of pounds on the Stock Exchange, from running a hairdressing salon to manufacturing car-engine parts.

Essentially business is the buying and selling of goods and services. A business woman is someone who is engaged in commercial or industrial activities, especially as an owner or executive, who aims to make profits. In this book the focus is on women entrepreneurs – that is, women who have set up their own business enterprises. We will also look at women at the other end of the business scale – those employed in business, such as clerical workers and secretaries who, in the 1930s, were called 'business girls'.

The effect that business women have had on the economy and on commercial life has remained largely uninvestigated by historians until quite recently. References to women in business can be found in old newspaper advertisements, town directories, accounts and court session papers. These references reveal that women have been engaged in a surprisingly wide variety of activities for many centuries, and show that it would be wrong to assume that women did not make an impact on the business world until the late twentieth century.

2

Early Business Women

My rest you'd disturb early in the morn
Leave me in bed comfortless and forlorn
Milk and water will not with me agree
Therefore I'll nothing have to do with thee.

A drawing of a country milk woman. Dairying and milk selling were businesses traditionally run by women.

Throughout history women have entered business for several reasons. It was socially acceptable for early business women who had been born into merchant families to become merchants themselves. For example, Rose of Burford, who died in 1330, was born into a family of London merchants. She built up a large, successful trade in wool and cloth, shipping wool overseas.

Many early business women had business thrust upon them by the death of their husband. Business widows were often unusually independent and they played an important part in the business world. After her merchant husband's death in 1470, Alice Chester developed a successful trade with Spain and Flanders, exporting cloth from Bristol and importing iron. She was also a generous benefactress, donating gifts to the Church and funding commercial ventures in Bristol. She herself died in 1485.

Numerous 'middle-class' women in Tudor and Stuart England (1485–1714) played an important role in commercial life. Isabella Tipping took over her husband's business – he was a leading Manchester linen draper – and for six years, up until her death in 1598, built it up until she was one of the wealthiest drapers in Manchester.

Some business women enjoyed a high profile. Elizabeth Calvert, who died in 1675, inherited one-third of her husband's estate when he died. (It was usual to give the other two-thirds to the Church and any children.) She took over his radical bookseller's business in the City of London. Over the years she was imprisoned several times for her views and was often in trouble for producing 'illegal' material. In 1667 she got into trouble for selling books to Susanna Moore, a bookseller in Bristol, which were 'likely to seduce persons' against the government. During her career as a bookseller she published books by many famous writers of the time.

While women were able to carry out a wide range of business activities, the legal position of married women was quite limited.

> **Oxford Flying Coach**
> **If any gentleman, or others, have occasion to ride to London in a coach, let them repair to the Three-Tun Tavern, where Places may be taken, to go from Oxford every Tuesday, Thursday and Saturday, and return from the Oxford-Arms in Warwick Lane, London, every Monday, Wednesday and Friday . . . The Price Ten Shillings, and each Passenger is allow'd to carry Six Pounds Weight. Perform'd (if God permit) by Anne Moore.**
> Lysons, *Collectanea*, ii, p.3.

A seventeenth-century shopping arcade showing women shopkeepers.

6 ▬▬▬▬▬▬

On 21 August 1789, *The World* carried an advertisement for a Mrs Knowles from Boulogne-Sur-Mer:

to inform the Nobility and Gentry, who frequent the English Hotel, that she has made some material improvements in her establishment. It is now, beyond comparison, the First Inn upon the Continent. The Fitting up of the home . . . the beds . . . the furniture, are all ENGLISH . . .

▬▬▬▬▬▬ 9

They were not, in effect, allowed to own property, and could not go to court for any kind of legal action in their own right without the agreement of their husbands.

In William Blackstone's *Commentaries*, published in 1765, he described married women's position: 'By marriage, the husband and wife are one person in law; that is, the very being or legal existence of the women is suspended during the marriage, or at least is incorporated and consolidated into that of the husband: under whose wing, protection, and cover she performs everything.' It is not surprising, then, to note the contrasting freedoms that the widow had, and indeed it is not at all surprising to find that so many business women were widows.

Newspapers, family accounts and institutional accounts all help to give us an idea of the wide variety of business activities that women were engaged in during the eighteenth century. Records from 1787 show that the Bristol Workhouse used women glaziers, pump makers, coal merchants, coffin makers and hatters. References to women stationers and booksellers are common. In London there were many profitable 'pamphlet

Left *A painting of a prosperous eighteenth-century shopkeeper from Glasgow. Enormous numbers of women ran their own shops.*

shops', which more often than not were run by women, that sold pamphlets, journals, newspapers, parliamentary speeches, almanacs and plays.

Women played an important part in selling perishable goods. Enormous numbers of women were in business as shopkeepers or street traders. There were many pedlars, fruit and vegetable sellers (who were mainly women) and street traders. Court session papers show that many women took out licences to trade as badgers. Badgers travelled from farm to farm buying eggs, milk, butter and corn, depending on their licences, which they then sold from door to door.

There are many instances of women hairdressers advertising in local papers and running their own businesses during the last quarter of the eighteenth century. Unfortunately many were put out of business when it became fashionable for one's hairdresser to be French and male.

Milliners ranked as the most important business women in the eighteenth century. The term milliner covered a wide variety of skills, including making cloaks, muffs, hoops, gloves, riding habits and petticoats. A five- to seven-year apprenticeship was required, and the capital needed by the apprentice to eventually set up in business might have been anything between £100 and £1,000, which was a fortune at the time. The larger businesses employed many 'outworkers', as needlework was a universal occupation for the poor who sewed at home for pitiful rates.

Below *An eighteenth-century trade card, advertising details of Mary and Ann Hogarth's dressmaking business.*

Mary & Ann Hogarth
from the Old Frock shop the corner of the Long Walk facing the Cloysters. Removed to ye Kings Arms joyning to ye Little Britain - gate near Long Walk Sells ye best & most Fashionable Ready Made Frocks, sutes of Fustian Ticken & Holland, stript Dimmity & Flanel Waftcoats, blue & canvas Frocks & bluecoat Boys Do. Likewise Fustians, Tickens, Hollands, white stript Dimitys, white & stript Flanels in ye piece by Wholefale or Retale, at Reafonable Rates.

3

Invisible Assets

1780–1850

The period 1780–1850 was a time of rapid economic, political and social change. During this period England was in a state of transition from a country where land was the major source of power, to an industrialist society with a new important middle class. By the middle of the nineteenth century, the middle classes included a large group of professionals and merchants in London, manufacturing families in the North and Midlands, market town tradesmen and also those in the 'service' industries – the auctioneers and agents, solicitors, farmers, designers, attorneys, bankers, scientists and engineers.

At the start of the period, home and business were strongly intertwined. Middle-class business families were often husband and wife teams, and most of the production was carried on in the home. The wife was the 'silent partner' – an invisible asset – who helped her husband to establish a successful commercial, manufacturing or professional enterprise.

A formidable-looking landlady. Running an inn was a very popular business activity because it allowed women to work at home.

'

Total amount for the two Alderneys made in the year, £50 6s 6d. My wife took for her hard labour in managing the two cows, £5 0s 0d, and I received £45 6s 6d, like all other lazy persons for doing nothing. Entry in an Essex farmer's diary, explaining how he benefited from his wife's cow-keeping. From *Family Fortunes* by L Davidoff and C Hall.

'

The family home and business were closely intertwined. Farmers' wives often used the front room of the house to run their own business.

Business men were usually surrounded by wives, sisters, daughters and women servants. Female relatives regularly took messages, witnessed wills, copied documents, and ordered supplies. One coach proprietor built up his business through the 'downright industry and a systematic application to business in which the female members of the family were called to assist.'

Some wives enjoyed the relative independence of running a business next door to their husband's. The farmer's wife might use the front room of the house as a small shop. Many women worked in the dressmaking and millinery business. In the late eighteenth century, sixteen of the nineteen retailers in Colchester were women. Ann Wilder starched muslin, lawn, gauze and lace. Mrs Courtney made muffs and Mary Waynman mended fans. These women ran their businesses independently. They took on apprentices and some made out bills in their own name.

Men often used women (their wives, sisters, daughters) to improve their businesses. Women's property and capital (a lump sum of money, or property) was regularly used to finance businesses. The marriage of daughters and sisters was arranged to enlarge contacts and sources of finance. A farming family of Corby arranged for all three daughters to marry Ipswich shopkeepers, thus ensuring a reliable outlet for their produce.

Family commitments influenced women's ability to function in business. The average woman had more than seven children, giving birth about every fourteen to twenty months. Some

> One man admiring the wealth and position of an illiterate Birmingham auctioneer noted that he was lucky enough to have a wife who: **conducted his correspondence, superintended his books, graced his hospital board and otherwise, by the ease and unaffected politeness of her demeanor, and the use of good, sound common sense, had contrived to make his name respected and his acquaintance deserved by men of all grades and people of all denominations.**
> From *Family Fortunes* by L Davidoff and C Hall.

> When George Courtald married Ruth Minton they lived off her marriage portion so that they could reinvest all the profits from their silk mill. She wrote to a friend about it saying: **I am no longer that useless, unconnected being lived only for herself, a burden to her friends.**

The marriage contract. Arranged marriages were extremely common in the eighteenth century. Daughters were often married off to further business connections.

> **She received the orders; made the purchases of materials; superintended the making of the goods; made out the accounts; and received the money besides taking care of her growing family. There were no 'Rights of Women' thought of in her day, but she was an entirely self-acting, managing mistress.**
>
> Description of a Mrs Holyoake, who ran a button workshop, by her son. From *Family Fortunes* by L Davidoff and C Hall.

women coped under remarkable pressure. Maria Savill, a young widow of an Essex builder, built up the family business while coping with ten children and two stepchildren!

Small investments held by women played an important part in the business world. Female capital financed the railway companies and other town amenities. Widows and spinsters were typical of those investors who liked safe investments such as annuities, which provided a fixed regular sum every year. Mrs Henstridge Cobbold from the Ipswich brewing family financed the local canal, rail, road and insurance companies and the Ipswich Gas Light Company.

With the new industrialization of the nineteenth century came private companies and large business corporations. Faced with this competition, small home-based businesses began to disappear, and this began the separation of family affairs from

It was important for a business man's reputation for him and his family to be seen to be regular churchgoers. During the nineteenth century business possibilities for women became severely restricted by ideas about morality and the home.

business. Home was now seen as a place of order and morality, away from the squalor of industry.

The behaviour of the entrepreneur and his wife and family was very important for a business man's reputation. Belonging to the local church or chapel was a good way of displaying one's morality. Towards the middle of the nineteenth century, hardening social expectations made it increasingly difficult for women to play a direct part in business and professional life.

The popular romantic idea of women was as the innocent dependant whom the male supported and protected. The husband produced and went into the outside world, his wife reproduced passively at home. Women had to uphold their status within the family and society by not being openly involved in business. Women might do 'male' work, but only behind closed doors as it would be taken as a sign of social inferiority. It was very difficult indeed for a woman to support herself on her own in this social climate. The consequences of these social pressures for those women who were left without the support of a man were serious.

The risk of a woman losing status if she was seen alone in many public places was a major disadvantage to women trying to do business. Women were not expected to be seen in markets and pubs where many business deals were transacted. In 1830 the behaviour of 'The Duchess', a female cattle dealer who sat with all the other dealers on market day in The Swan pub smoking her pipe and drinking, was considered very eccentric.

In the late eighteenth century many women ran inns. Perhaps this was acceptable because the inn was the family home and much of the brewing was done on the premises. Inns often

Many women innkeepers were colourful characters who ran their businesses with great energy and efficiency.

doubled up as coaching businesses, and sold or hired tools. In the 1790s, Deborah Gooding ran the successful Essex to London route. In the Essex area a Mrs Warren also dealt in blacksmithing equipment, and a Mrs Sergeant contracted out threshing machines from her pub.

In the early nineteenth century, changes in the brewing industry began to push women out of the business. By 1800 many public houses were being bought up by the large breweries. Male managers, clerks and agents were preferred. Women who owned, managed or worked in public houses went against the grain of public opinion. Lucrative coaching businesses began to fail with the arrival of the railways. By the middle of the century, women's traditional connection with transport businesses was broken.

In farming, too, women's traditional jobs were being lost through the introduction of steam-powered machinery, larger farms and larger work-forces. These factors, combined with the prevailing social climate, meant that middle-class young, unmarried women were removed from contact with the mainly male work-force. Traditionally dairying was a business concern which involved the farmer's wife, her daughters, nieces, sisters and live-in dairy maids. But now dairying activities declined. By 1843 the Royal Commission on Women and Children in Agriculture stated that the patience, skill and strength needed to produce cheese made this work unsuitable for women!

The Industrial Revolution brought important changes. The arrival of steam-powered machinery in farming meant that many jobs traditionally done by women began to disappear.

4

The Victorian Era

1837–1901

During the eighteenth century women had been slowly moving away from participating actively in commerce, farming and other business activities. The historian Ivy Pinchbeck, in *Women Workers and the Industrial Revolution*, explains how, in the nineteenth century, the Industrial Revolution affected women in business. 'In the past, marriage for many women had been some sort of business partnership in agriculture, trade or domestic industry, but in the reorganization which accompanied the

Charity was thought a very fitting activity for well-to-do Victorian women.

'
. . . ladies, dismissed from the dairy, the confectionery, the store room, the still room, the poultry yard, the kitchen garden, and the orchard have hardly yet found themselves a sphere equally useful and important in the pursuits of trade and art to which to apply their too abundant leisure.
Entry in Margaretta Greg's diary in 1853, from *Memoir of John Greg* by J E Butler.
'

The Victorians did not consider any work which involved making profit suitable for women. Charity was their 'proper' calling. Here a wealthy woman visits a family living in slum conditions.

> *Many young prostituted females from the polish of their manners, and from the history they relate, must have had respectable origin: and they have become prey to this vice through their inability to procure an employment suited to their capacities, and the impulses of sheer want.*
> From an article in the *Pamphleteer* in 1827.

Prostitution has always been one form of 'business' for women.

Industrial Revolution, the majority of married women lost their economic independence. Unless they became wage earners outside the home, like factory workers, they were financially dependent on their husbands.' She compares the 'vigorous life of the eighteenth-century business woman, travelling about the country in her own interests,' with 'the sheltered existence of the Victorian woman.'

The Victorians attached considerable prestige to being a 'lady of leisure', and the numbers of well-to-do women in mercantile and commercial enterprises fell. Margaretta Greg wrote in her diary in 1853: 'A lady, to be such, must be a mere lady, and nothing else. She must not work for profit, or engage in any occupation that money can command, lest she invade the rights of the working classes, who live by their labour.'

One occupation that was considered a proper activity for a 'lady' was charity work. Many women worked energetically at

> **Plain needlework done at home is so ill-paid that almost the worst kind of servant's place is preferable to this employment . . . 30,000 women live by this trade in London alone . . . Life on these terms is not life, but a slow death.**
> From 'On the choice of a business' by Jessie Boucherett, in *The English Woman's Journal*, 1 November 1862.

Working in factories was thought to be unsuitable for 'genteel' women. Home-based industries like lace-making started up so that women could be at home while earning a living.

it. In H. More's *Coelebs in Search of a Wife*, published in 1809, Miss Stanley says, 'I have often heard it regretted, that ladies have no stated employment, no profession. It is a mistake. Charity is the calling of a lady; the care of the poor is her profession.'

Many working-class women found employment in the growing number of factories, but in so doing they were criticized for being bad mothers and housewives. The government reports of the 1830s and 1840s presented working wives as unnatural and immoral, and suggested that married women who *had* to enter paid employment should work at home where they could not be seen.

This harsh social climate left many single 'genteel' ladies in distressing circumstances – without income and without respectable paid employment. One result of this was the development of new domestic industries, such as lace-making, straw plaiting, and glove and button making. Taking in lodgers provided a livelihood for many widows and other women left without support, and some unmarried women ran schools for a living.

In the second half of the nineteenth century there was a revolution in retailing. Consumer goods, like clothes and food, started to be mass-produced, and shops increased in size. The wholesaler and large-scale manufacturer now did the work previously done by the small retailer, like grading, sorting, weighing, and packing. Small family shops began to close and larger scale operations flourished. Chains of shops and department stores came into their own.

Lewis's department store in Liverpool was one of the many new department stores of the Victorian era.

'

Jessie Boucherett advised daughters of business men to serve in their father's shops because: *. . . if she have no brother, or if he enters some other profession, she will then be able to succeed her father in the business, and will know how to carry it on. This is sometimes done, but not so often as it ought to be . . . A girl should always consider it a great advantage to be taught her father's trade.*
From *The English Woman's Journal*, 1 November 1862.

,

The 1870 Elementary Education Act ruled that all children should receive an elementary education, and this was now the only training that was needed to become a shop assistant. Women shop assistants began to arrive in their droves, providing cheap and efficient labour. By 1914 they numbered close to half a million. Their wages were half those of men employed in the same shop, and were further eroded by fines for unpunctuality, business errors, and even for allowing a customer to leave without making a purchase!

In the mid-nineteenth century women began to demand higher education and training. Women agitated to be admitted into industry and the professions. Jessie Boucherett, in connection with the Society for Promoting the Employment of Women,

ALL THE DIFFERENCE!

Haberdasher (to Assistant who has had the "swop"). "WHY HAS THAT LADY GONE WITHOUT BUYING?"
Assistant. "WE HAVEN'T GOT WHAT SHE WANTS."
Haberdasher. "I'LL SOON LET YOU KNOW, MISS, THAT I KEEP YOU TO SELL WHAT I'VE GOT, AND NOT WHAT PEOPLE WANT!"

began classes to prepare girls for commercial careers. She attributed the cause of the misery of unemployed women to: 'the neglect of parents to apprentice their daughters to some trade or handicraft as regularly as they do their sons.'

The Civil Service changed in response to the rapidly expanding industrial and urban economy, making the employment of educated middle-class women essential. The most important government department was the Post Office which expanded its services. It was the first government department to employ women clerical workers. The number of its employees increased sixfold between 1851 and 1891, and doubled between 1891 and 1914. By 1914 the Post Office was the largest business organization in England, and the greatest single employer of middle-class women in Britain. In 1881 women sorters were introduced and recruited through open, competitive exams.

In 1876 the women's clerical branch of the Post Office was organized under the command of Maria Constance Smith. At

Thousands of unskilled women worked in the new large stores. They earned half as much as male shop assistants, and were sometimes fined if a customer failed to make a purchase!

Women Post Office workers in the General Post Office in London around 1895.

the age of twenty-three she was appointed the Lady Superintendent, and in the ensuing thirty-seven years built the staff up from 40 to 2,000. She was dedicated to making the government's decision to employ women a great success.

In 1893 two women factory inspectors were appointed. They faced a great deal of prejudice. Men considered their appointment a 'terrible proposition' because 'the women would get their petticoats in the machines'. It was 'unseemly that they should go about alone at night in the workshops.' The first woman inspector in the Civil Service was Mrs Jane Elizabeth Senior, who was appointed the inspector of workhouse schools in 1874. Her special enquiry reported on the education of pauper girls, and she came up against much criticism from members of the board for her recommendations regarding the Poor Law. Adelaide Anderson (later Dame Adelaide), was in charge of the Woman's Branch of the Factory Department in 1894. She worked there for twenty-four years, dealing with complaints and investigating the condition of women and children in industry.

In almost all departments of the Civil Service women earned less than men. Their prospects were limited. Women did not move up the grades automatically as men did. There was also the problem of the marriage bar – a law that prevented married women from working. In 1875 the Post Office ruled that in future only single women and widows would be employed. Women who married were compelled to leave the service.

In the Victorian era many women lost the opportunity to earn a living, and marriage for middle-class women became the only way to survive. Around the turn of the twentieth century women did begin to move towards greater economic independence. The Married Women's Property Act of 1882 had far-reaching social effects. For the first time in England, married women were granted the rights of separate ownership of every kind of property. The 1882 act was extended in 1893 by an act which put a married woman and her property on the same footing as a single woman. These acts, the drive for women to arm themselves with education, and the agitation for admission of women in industry, meant that women could begin again to take their rightful place in the business world.

A woman factory inspector visits a sweatshop at the turn of the century. The first women factory inspectors were appointed in 1893.

The number of women clerks working in large business offices rose sharply at the turn of the century.

❝
No girl should be allowed to enter the profession until she is old enough to protect herself, should the need arise, from the undesirable employer, who may insult her with unwelcome attentions.
Advice by the Women's Association in 1913 in relation to the need for a minimum educational qualification.
❞

5

New Business for Women

1900–1945

One area of employment for women in business that expanded greatly at the turn of the century was in clerical (office) work. Growing industrial and commercial enterprises, like banking and advertising, meant that business offices increased in size and the number of clerical workers multiplied in industry, trade and in enterprises such as banking, insurance, publishing and advertising.

Between 1861 and 1911, the number of male clerks increased fivefold, and the number of women clerks increased four hundred times! Some attributed the increase in women clerks to the arrival of the typewriter, saying that typing was like playing the piano, thus making it an instrument especially suited to women's abilities!

Machines for sorting, stamping, calculating and sealing were introduced at the turn of the century. Filing, bookkeeping, and record departments were set up. The typing pools in offices resembled factories. Men were considered the main wage earners who had to support their families, and were paid more

The typewriter helped women into businesses, but only in support roles. Typing was considered particularly suited to women's abilities.

than women for doing the same job. The average earnings for men in insurance companies between 1910 and 1914 were 53s 6d, and for women 23s. Women had little prospect of rising to more interesting, responsible and well-paid jobs, largely because the marriage bar still dictated that paid employment was likely to be a short-lived episode in their lives.

Between 1914 and 1918, as men were called up to fight in the First World War, women began, informally, to play a more prominent role in business once again. During this period there were a number of successful women independent entrepreneurs. Margaret Haig Thomas (Viscountess Rhonda) was already a successful business woman by the time of the First World War through participating in her father's mining business. She eventually started and also financed the publishing venture that produced the *Time and Tide* magazine in 1920, the feminist political weekly magazine which gave women an independent voice.

At the end of the war, many women retained their clerical jobs, but the return of thousands of men to civilian life forced

It is no use men burying their heads in the sand and saying Women's Place is not in the Office.
Comment by an early trade union leader.

Some women clerical workers did try to complain about their unequal treatment, as shown in this Punch *cartoon from 1908.*

Lady Clerk. "YES, THEY ACTUALLY COMPLAINED IN THE OFFICE TO-DAY BECAUSE WE WERE TALKING TOO MUCH. THEY WOULDN'T DO THAT IF WE WERE MEN!"

another 750,000 women to leave paid employment. The general manager of a shipping company, on replacing wartime women workers with ex-servicemen, said: 'After all a girl's idea is marriage, so is it not better to employ the future bread-winners who will marry them some day?'

In 1918 women over the age of thirty won the vote. The Sex Disqualification (Removal) Act of 1919 followed, which, among many other things, forced the Institute of Chartered Accountants to open its doors to their first woman member, Mary Harris Smith. Despite this act, in 1927 the *Evening Standard* reported a Miss Woodman, the director and general manager of a bookbinding company, as saying: 'I have found sex prejudice everywhere I have been in business.'

During the inter-war period, single women were recruited into the clerical jobs in banks, in private firms and in state-controlled businesses. They became buyers, auctioneers, accountants, insurance agents and shipping agents. According to the *Westminster Gazette* in May 1926, a Miss Jeffryes was the best-known shipping agent in London. Another great entrepreneur during this period was Daisy Hyams, who started trading with Jack Cohen by selling cheap market goods from the backs of lorries. They set up Tesco, which in time grew to be the massive concern it is today.

Despite coming across prejudice, business women moved with determination into all areas of the market-place. In 1924 the *Daily Mail* reported that a 'blue-eyed girl', a Miss Constance Wilkins, had invaded the 'stronghold of City masculine autocracy' by setting up offices in the City and specializing in buying spices from abroad. Because no woman was allowed to be a member of the commercial salesrooms of the City, she had to do her buying through a broker. In 1925 there were only five women members of the London Chamber of Commerce. In 1928 there were nearly two hundred.

In 1926 Miss Gordon Holmes, the managing director of the National Securities Corporation, one of the largest financial houses in London, was the only woman stockbroker in the country. She started work as a typist during the war, earning £1.00 per week, and she got a job in a financial business in the City. She recalls how, when she asked her employer questions about the business, he answered: 'With all due respect to women, the female mind is not capable of understanding finance.' She said, 'Years afterwards when I ran his business for him I reminded him of these words.'

There were plenty of opportunities for women in the financial world, but it was difficult for them to obtain the necessary

> *I am surprised that so much fuss is made when a woman occupying an important commercial or administrative position comes into prominence. It must be because people do not realise the great number of women who are holding responsible positions today. Real 'equality' will have been reached when we cease to regard with amazement a woman who has done anything particularly well!*
>
> Quote from Miss Woodman, *Sunday Times*, 4 September 1927.

> *I was living in a hostel in Vauxhall Bridge Road which was run for single business ladies . . . they were the smallest rooms I've ever inhabited . . . there was just room for a bed and a little tiny sort of gangway and a chest of drawers . . . you had breakfast every day and all meals at the weekend . . . and your laundry . . . for 30s a week. That was half my wages.*
>
> Woman's description of the hostel she lived in during the late 1930s.

In the 1920s women moved into some of the top buying positions in large London stores, such as Harrods.

experience. Many started by doing office work and then trying to set up business on their own, but they often faced further prejudice when trying to raise capital.

Between the wars women were also succeeding in other male-dominated areas of the business world. The *Woman's Leader* reported in 1931 that a woman director of a firm of granite engineers and general merchants was also a member of the Institute of Quarrying, and the London representative for *The Quarry Managers' Journal*, *Good Roads*, *Cement, Lime and Gravel* and other such papers.

During this period there were more openings for top jobs in the retail trade. In 1924 an article in *The Lady* about women buyers reported that, 'Almost any department is now open to a woman, though millinery, dresses, mantles and underlinen afford her the best opportunities.' Women in the 1930s became directors of large London stores. Sir Woodman Burbridge, chairperson of Harrods said: 'I have the greatest respect for women in business . . . I also believe that in big stores all articles which are exclusively for women should be purchased and sold by women. Women buyers are essential in stores like Harrods.'

Women were also employed in managerial experiments. Miss Laura Bowen was general manager for Peter Jones in March 1930, where about twenty women graduates were undergoing special training to become saleswomen or buyers. There were also increasing openings for women in the retail trade's 'Home

6

Buying is a very complex operation but, in spite of the detail and the problems, which are many because of seasonal factors and delivery delays and so on, the objective has to be simple and well defined . . . Our computer is an invaluable aid – we use it but it does not dominate us when judgements involving consumer preference can depend on personal experience and feel for products.
Daisy Hyams in *Pile it High and Sell it Cheap* by Maurice Corina.

9

Service'. Many gas, electricity and industrial firms extended their home service departments to include salespeople who called door to door, to give demonstrations and help the customer 'get the best out of materials and apparatus she buys for use in her home.'

Even more than the First World War, the Second World War (1939–45) brought with it increased employment for women. In 1945, 34 per cent of the labour force in engineering was female. Shortly before the Second World War, the government officially accepted a policy of common seniority lists for the Civil Service, which meant that work was interchangeable between men and women. The marriage bar had been modified during the inter-war years, and it was temporarily suspended during the Second World War. This opened the way for agitation for its removal. The marriage bar was finally removed in teaching in 1944, and in the Civil Service in 1946.

The number of working women rose significantly during the Second World War, particularly in engineering industries.

Daisy Hyams (b. 1902)

After leaving school, Daisy Hyams spent a brief spell working for a tailor's, before starting as an assistant bookkeeper and clerk at John Cohen's food warehouse in Upper Clapton Road, London. Daisy proved to be a dedicated worker. She would be there doing office work at midnight after the Christmas traders had come and all the vans were loaded up. Early on there were signs of her great organizational skill. She found, for example, that customers were being charged a different price for the same goods, so she replaced the quotations, which were glued in an old exercise book, with a proper costing file.

Daisy became directly involved in the growth of the business and became one of John Cohen's closest friends. She worked ceaselessly behind the scenes, helping him to realize his vision of using the cut-price selling techniques of market stall holders in a string of 'conventional' high street shops. He opened his first store in 1929, and by 1932 own-brand lines were introduced and the Tesco name appeared, with the shops operating under the slogan 'Tesco Stores – the Modern Grocers'.

In the mid-1930s Daisy moved into 'Tesco House' as John Cohen's personal assistant. The new premises incorporated offices, distributing warehouses and the first modern food warehouse in the country. She worked closely with John Cohen and became, as she says, a 'jack of all trades'. By the time of the Second World War there were about 100 shops in the chain. In 1948 there were about 10 of the new 'help-yourself' Tesco in Britain, and by 1960 about 6,000. As Tesco grew, so did Daisy's valuable experience and expertise, and by 1967 she was buying controller.

By 1971 Daisy Hyams was managing director of Tesco Wholesale Limited, controlling an expenditure of around £3 million a week. Her individual flair and initiative helped to make the complex, computer-programmed food buying operation a highly successful concern. Daisy Hyams retired at the age of seventy, but remains firmly rooted in the business world that she dedicated her life to, and still acts as a consultant for the Tesco chain.

Daisy Hyams, managing director of Tesco during the 1970s.

Equal rights campaigners in London in 1971. The Women's Liberation Movement has helped many women to get on in the business world.

6

The Post-War Years

1945–1969

In the years immediately after the war, women were once again encouraged to believe that being a wife and mother was a worthwhile full-time career. In the 1950s, however, there followed an acute shortage of labour, and women were suddenly encouraged back into waged work.

Many working women in the 1950s and 1960s recognized that they were just being used as a temporary work-force, to be drawn into the job market, or dropped, according to men's needs. They wanted to do something to protect women's position in the employment market, and this in part led to the rise of the Women's Liberation Movement in the late 1960s. The Women's Liberation Movement brought many issues to the public eye, and vigorously campaigned for changes in the law

Mary Quant, business woman and fashion designer, was one of the most influential minds behind the fashion scene in the 1960s. Part of her success lay in designing clothes that were within the price range of fashionable teenagers.

In June 1970 a group of women journalists stormed one of the last Fleet Street male strongholds, El Vino's wine bar. The Women's Liberation Movement led hundreds of women to strike out against sexual discrimination.

to relieve women of some of the discrimination against them in the workplace.

Between 1911 and 1951 there had been a depressingly slow increase in the number of women in top positions in the job market. Women had 6 per cent of jobs in top professions in 1911, but still only 8 per cent in 1951. Women in the business world were still concentrated at the lower end of the scale, but opportunities and openings for women in business did grow as women's experience of business broadened.

In the 1960s, women armed with good qualifications were competing on an equal footing with men for some of the top jobs in the financial world. Sexual discrimination against women was still rife, but gradually women's experience and expertise in the financial world was growing. There were now women financial analysts and women moving into some of the top posts at the Bank of England. Scotland admitted its first woman

Stock Market guides. In 1963 women were allowed into the London Stock Exchange gallery – but only as guides, to give talks to visitors and show them round!

6 ▬▬▬▬▬▬

Why should the City be so set against women? Nearly half the money handled on the stock exchange belongs to women – and more than half the country's spending each year is done by women.
Evening Standard, at the height of the controversy over women joining the Stock Exchange.
▬▬▬▬▬▬ 9

6 ▬▬▬▬▬▬

I am quite prepared to meet the Council half-way by giving a firm undertaking never actually to enter the trading floor.
Elizabeth Rivers-Bulkeley, during her fight to become a member of the stock market, 1962.
▬▬▬▬▬▬ 9

stockbroker in 1964. Meanwhile in England, Elizabeth Rivers-Bulkeley, who was a stockbroker working in one of the largest stockbroking firms in the country, fought to become the first woman on the Stock Exchange. Membership of the Stock Exchange enabled women to become partners in their firm, sharing the profits instead of handing over most of their commission.

In January 1967, the Stock Exchange Council agreed in principle to consider the admission of women as members – but then added that the women would not be admitted to the floor of the house during business hours. The reasons given by stockbrokers for excluding women were, they 'would never fit in', they were not 'as decisive as men', and that men 'couldn't relax' if women were there!

At this time the chairperson of the Stock Exchange estimated that there were about three million women shareholders, and Inland Revenue returns showed that women had bigger holdings than men in ordinary shares, gilt-edged stock, building societies and Post Office trustee savings accounts. A group of about twenty women were only finally elected to membership with effect from the 25 March 1973. One of them, Susan Shaw, claims to have been the first woman to set foot on the floor of the Stock Exchange.

In the 1960s Elizabeth Pepperell, who was the assistant director of the Industrial Society (which offers training and advice to

One of the first women members on the floor of the Stock Exchange, 26 March 1973.

the business world), pioneered work to improve the position of women. She offered courses, organized conferences, and helped organizations with their individual problems. By improving training policies and promotion procedures she heightened people's awareness of the need for equal opportunities for women in business. In 1962 there were no woman directors on the boards of banks or insurance companies, but the number of women in top jobs in the financial world was increasing dramatically. By 1967 Irene Kuhn was the managing director of Rea Brothers, a leading merchant bank. At Barclays Bank there were three female branch managers and two women assistant general managers at head office. There were women on the boards of three unit trust management companies, and there was even a woman City editor of *The Times*.

6

There was no precedent for the work I was to do. I had to create my own programme.
Elizabeth Pepperell, on moving to her new job as assistant director of the Industrial Society.

9

Elizabeth Pepperell (1915–69)

Elizabeth Pepperell was born during the First World War. She was one of a family of seven who lived in the East End of London. She left school at the age of fourteen to work as a match-packer at Bryant and May, the local match factory. She became a supervisor and joined the union. After attending some lectures on industrial history she decided to go to evening classes in economics. She went on to apply for, and was awarded, a Mary MacArthur Scholarship, which enabled her to leave the factory to study social sciences at the London School of Economics.

She began her career in personnel work soon after the outbreak of the Second World War, as a chief welfare officer. In 1952 Elizabeth Pepperell became assistant director of the Industrial Society, a registered charity which offers training and advice in all areas of the business world. She concentrated on improving working conditions in the retail trade, in banks, offices and in hospitals.

She worked hard for equal opportunities for women in business, organizing her first all-women conference in the summer of 1952. In the 1960s she launched a five-day course for women in responsible positions. It was always fully booked. She led the Industrial Society's work into the commercial field, and today much of its work is done in the City of London, with banks and other commercial institutions. She also served on many government committees and working parties.

In 1963 Elizabeth Pepperell became ill, and was told that she had only fifteen months to live. Despite her illness, she courageously

Elizabeth Pepperell was dedicated to achieving equal opportunities for women in business.

struggled through the next six years, and continued to work as best as she could, often dictating letters from her hospital bed. She did not live to see the Equal Pay Act in 1970, a year after her death. The Sex Discrimination Act followed in 1975. Both acts were in some way the results of her dedicated pioneering work for women. In 1984 the Pepperell Unit was launched by the Industrial Society to help improve women's conditions at work.

7

Female Entrepreneurs

1970–1990

During the 1970s, changes in Britain's economy had far-reaching effects on the labour force, and thus on women's involvement in the business world. The computer industry was growing fast, new technology was appearing in many industries, and there was rising unemployment. Serious job shortages, and the closure of pre-school child-care facilities due to lack of money, meant that many women were forced to stay at home.

A number of government measures such as the 1970 Equal Pay Act and the 1975 Sex Discrimination Act and Employment Protection Act, did attempt to help female employees. But despite these measures, economic recession made it very difficult for women to break down the traditional barriers to working in typically male jobs.

Today, women make up nearly half the total work-force and yet they are still crowded into a narrow sector of stereotyped female occupations. A quarter of employed women work in the manufacturing industries, and of these half work in the four

The introduction of computers into businesses in the 1970s had important consequences for the job market.

The chart below shows how few women there are in top jobs. Discrimination still stops some women from being promoted beyond a certain level at work.

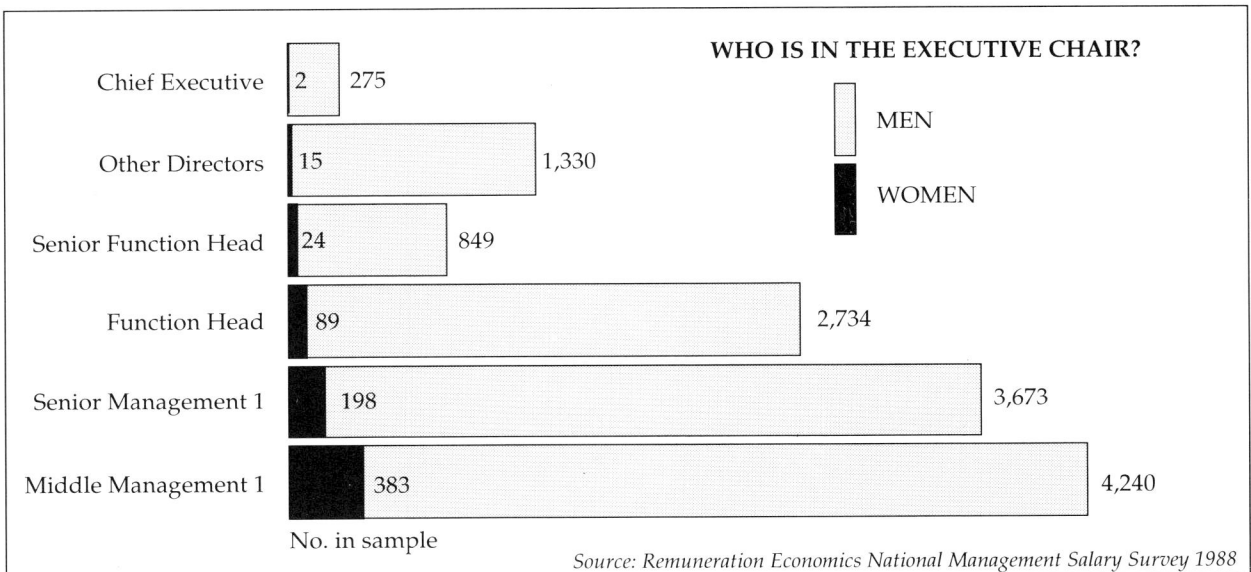

WHO IS IN THE EXECUTIVE CHAIR?

MEN

WOMEN

	Women	Men
Chief Executive	2	275
Other Directors	15	1,330
Senior Function Head	24	849
Function Head	89	2,734
Senior Management	198	3,673
Middle Management	383	4,240

No. in sample

Source: Remuneration Economics National Management Salary Survey 1988

A quarter of employed women work in the manufacturing industries, often in low paid, part-time jobs.

industries of food and drink manufacture, footwear, textiles and electrical engineering. Others work in the service industries, which include catering, laundry, nursing, clerical work and shops. Women are concentrated in the less secure, lower paid, part-time occupations with higher levels of staff turnover.

When women are prevented, through discrimination, from reaching beyond a certain level at work, they are said to have hit the 'glass ceiling'. This invisible barrier causes a great deal of frustration to women in management. In addition to outright discrimination, women also suffer from low expectations. When most directors in a company are men, it is harder for young women to have the confidence to push themselves to the top.

Perhaps it is not surprising that there are so few women in top jobs in the business world when we look at women's dual roles as domestic workers and members of the labour force. In 1977 nine million women worked outside their homes; over one-third worked part-time. Women's role in the work-force and family size are closely connected. Having children often determines whether or not a woman is able to work outside the home in business. Women tend to drop out of the labour market after the birth of their first child. British women come up against a shortage of professional child-minders, crèches and child-care facilities. In Britain in the late 1980s, less than 2 per cent of children under three years of age received child care, whereas in Denmark the figure was 40 per cent. Child-care

'*Why are there so few business women? I think it is this fear of risk-taking . . . It is psychologically suggested that the whole concept of women's role is one of nurturing and, therefore, it's not risk-taking.* A business woman. '

The shortage of child-care facilities in Britain causes enormous problems for working women.

'

Women should be able to choose to spend time with their children without sacrifice of their career or self in the process.
Steve Shirley, cited in *Women Mean Business* by Veronica Groocock.

'

Women executives are still paid less than male equivalents. However, female managers tend to be younger than their male peers, which may account for the difference in earnings.

expenses are not allowed to be set against income tax. Some women find that running their own business is one of their reasons for deciding not to have any more children.

There are some women entrepreneurs who provide an excellent example to other prospective business women, and who have made their mark by changing some of the more difficult work practices for women. Steve Shirley is the founder director of the FI Group, which designs, manufactures and installs computer systems. Women in FI work a minimum of twenty-five hours per week, but as their children become older and more independent they can 'grow' their careers by increasing their working hours. Computer systems link the homes of about 300 managers and all FI's offices and work centres.

More organizations now recognize that the career paths for men and women are different, and that to get ahead women need special help to develop their skills and confidence. There are courses designed to help women to be more assertive. Other courses are available on the management of conflict and stress, managing career breaks, self-development, risk-taking, decision-making, and coping with company politics.

The business woman's image can play an important part in her success, and there are courses on identity and image. Vivien Padwick is the chairperson and managing director of Vivair, a company she launched in 1978, which is now the second-largest

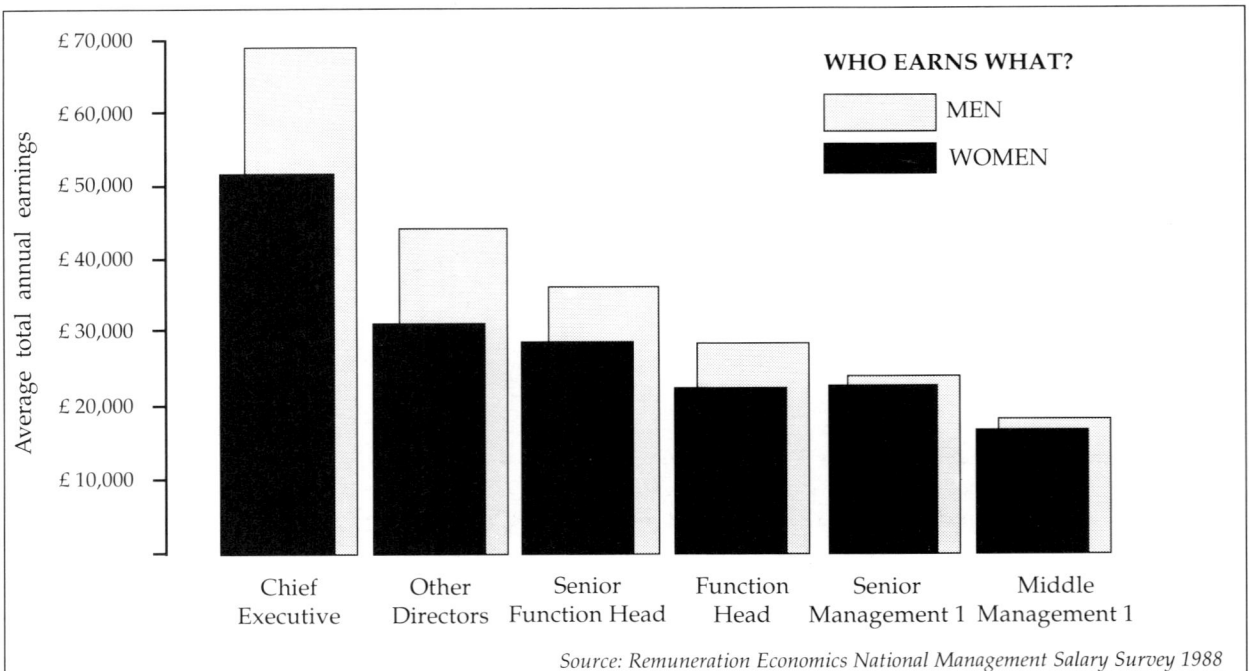

WHO EARNS WHAT?

MEN
WOMEN

Source: Remuneration Economics National Management Salary Survey 1988

Women barristers at work. During the 1970s and 1980s the number of women entering the legal professions rose. There are now more academically qualified women to compete for jobs.

air charter broker in Britain and has a turnover of about £20 million. She maintains that, 'If you are trying to get up the ladder, the first thing you do is to dress the part. I've always dressed as if I was an executive'. In many businesses women do find that how they dress affects the way they are treated.

There are now more academically qualified women competing for higher managerial and professional occupations. Between 1971 and 1980, the percentage of females at the Chartered Insurance Institute rose from 4 per cent to 10 per cent, as did the number of women at the Institute of Bankers. In 1986–7, for the first time more women than men passed the Solicitor's final examinations. However, women are promoted less often than male colleagues with similar qualifications, and have to fight to prove themselves to be 'career minded'.

'
. . . in the closing month of 1986 the Institute of Directors reported that out of the top 100 UK companies, only nine had women directors.
From the introduction to the *Directory of Women Directors.*
'

'
Business presents a special opportunity for women. Traditionally, with a few distinguished exceptions, it has been the preserve of men. Today, the realization is growing – and growing fast – that women possess, in abundance, just the right blend of character to succeed in business.
Michael Grylls MP, chairman of the Small Business Bureau.
'

Steve Shirley (b. 1933)

Steve Shirley is a mathematics graduate who started work in 1951 as a statistician for the Post Office Research Station. In 1959 she moved into computing with ICL and became a senior analyst. She left in 1962 expecting her first child and was struck by the unnecessary waste of talent caused by women leaving the labour market at the peak of their performance to have children.

Wanting to continue her career, Steve Shirley set up her own one-woman firm called Freelance Programmers Ltd, and

Steve Shirley

started signing herself 'Steve' as it got her interviews with prospective clients. With entrepreneurial flair, she foresaw the explosion there was going to be in computing services, and she brought in women in similar positions to herself to work with her.

Her company, where she still operates as founder director, is now called the FI Group. It is an information systems company which designs computer systems to suit their clients' needs. Then they develop, build and install them. Some of their clients are Access, the National Westminster Bank, Tesco and the Department of Transport.

Steve Shirley evolved her own working environment. The company now employs 1,000 people, the majority of whom are women who work at home or in a network of local work centres, all designed around where the work-force live. A core of key jobs at head office work a conventional nine-to-five day, but most of the work-force including programmers, analysts, business consultants, sales force and a marketing team have their own flexible work scheme. Such organization allows skilled computing professionals to continue and enhance their careers in a flexible working environment.

Steve Shirley was awarded an OBE for her services to industry in 1980. She is the first woman president of the British Computer Society, and serves on Lord Young's committee for the National Council for Vocational Qualifications. She is on the council of the Industrial Society and is a Companion of the British Institute of Management. She is also a member of the Council for the City University Business School. She lists one of her interests in *Who's Who* as 'sleep'!

8

Encouraging Women into Business

The importance of encouraging women into business has only recently been recognized. The major development for women has been a growth in the number of networks – organizations rather like societies or clubs – which get business women to help each other by exchanging skills, know-how and business contacts. Networks are a good example of a male practice that has been very usefully adopted by women in business.

Being a member of a network is useful for business women who want to move into a higher position in their own field because information on job vacancies, useful telephone numbers, key contacts in certain organizations and information about training and conferences is available to members. Some networks are company-based like at British Telecom and Shell, while others cover wider areas of business, for example Women in Management, and the Women's Enterprise Development Agency (WEDA). Many are professionally-based, for example

Networks such as Women into Business provide vital information and support for business women.

> ❝ *It is my duty to help create a new breed of women, who accept success as a way of life. Otherwise my own achievements will be just an invisible microdot on the map.* Ellen Gordon, the Chicagan sweet manufacturer with a turnover exceeding $200 million. ❞

SUCCESSFUL APPLICANTS (BY SEX) TO THE ENTERPRISE ALLOWANCE SCHEME, 1983 - 7

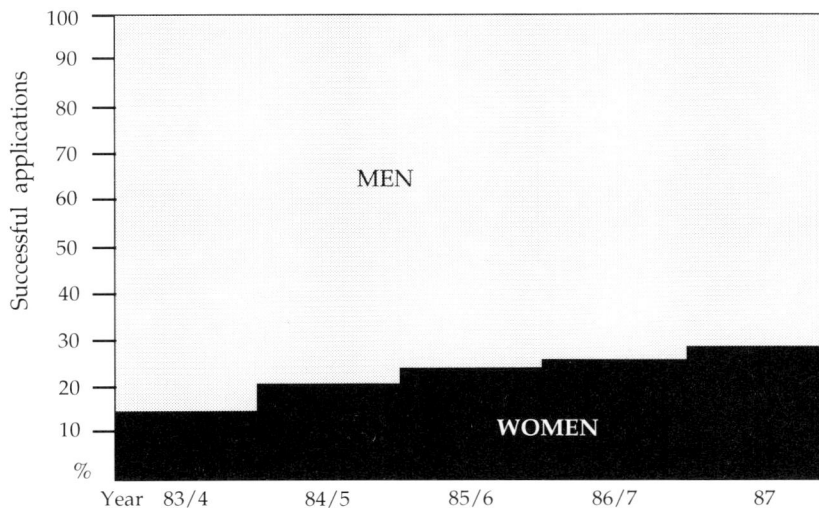

Source: Manpower Services Commission

Statistics show that enterprise schemes are beginning to encourage more women to start their own businesses.

networks like Women in Banking or Women into Engineering, Science and Technology.

The Confederation of British Industry (CBI) reported that during the period 1983–7 nearly twice as many men as women were seeking opportunities for self-employment. The government's Enterprise Allowance Scheme was set up to encourage people into business by offering financial backing to those starting up. Unfortunately the CBI has not yet obtained statistics on the number of applications by women, but it points out that women, 'may be discouraged from applying because of the requirement to demonstrate their access to capital', an area in which women still come up against discrimination.

The Small Business Bureau, which lobbies Parliament for better conditions for small businesses, decided that there was not enough encouragement for women to choose business as a career and very little information about the advantages of business ownership for women who wanted to combine their lives as mothers and wives with a rewarding career. In 1986 it set up the network 'Women into Business', which works to give successful business women a higher national profile. It set up a counselling service so that successful entrepreneurs could assist new women entrepreneurs and help them avoid typical pitfalls. It also organizes teach-ins, seminars and conferences for business women.

One theory is that more women would be encouraged into business if successful business women were given greater publicity. High profile, successful business women are role models who are an inspiration to others. Laura Ashley, for example, set up a business which developed into the chain of shops named after her. She is an example of a woman who successfully merged her home and her business life. Laura Ashley started in 1953, printing textiles from her London flat. As her designs sold, her company expanded. Between 1953 and 1985 she and her family lived in ten different houses. New designs that fitted in with the period of each house found their way into her shops. Her success provides inspiration to other women who might feel they have a good, marketable idea.

In recent years business awards have been set up to encourage women into business, resulting from the concern that women at the top of the business world had no high-profile role models to inspire them. The awards are given to women who have power, charisma, dynamism, innovation and tenacity. Achievement, style, the ability to motivate, along with business acumen and enterprise are all considered important qualities.

The 'Veuve Clicquot Business Woman of the Year' award

There is a need to promote positive but accessible role models for women going into business . . . The concentration upon a few highly successful women, however, could act as a disincentive to many prospective entrepreneurs. Greater coverage of a larger number of different and identifiable women whose achievements are more accessible might act as a spur for other women.

From a study of female business owners by Sarah Carter and Tom Cannon for the Department of Employment, (Research Paper No. 65).

Leah Hertz was a law academic and a talented designer. She formed her own international group of companies, including the knitwear firm of Crochetta. As a successful business woman she gave much time and expertise to prospective business women. She ran seminars and was editor of the magazine Women into Business.

started in 1972 to celebrate Veuve Clicquot, the French widow who built up the highly successful champagne business after her husband's death in 1712. She even beat Napoleon's blockade to supply the Russian court with their favourite champagne. Stella Brumell won the first British award in 1973 when it was called, significantly, 'A Woman in a Man's World' award. She was the chairperson of a firm in Warwick making concrete-mixing machinery. A review of the winners since then reveals some of the biggest names in women's business, such as Debbie Moore (founder, chairperson and managing director of Pineapple Studios), Sophie Mirman (chairperson and joint managing

Mair Barnes, managing director of Woolworths, won the Business Woman of the Year Award in 1989. Mair Barnes had moved the company from a loss of £4 million to a profit of £45 million in two years.

director of Sock Shop International), and Mair Barnes (managing director of Woolworths).

Aspiring business women often come up against gender-related problems when trying to start their business. Getting a loan from the bank can prove difficult when bank managers tend not to take business women seriously. In the end, many business women are forced to take a male partner along. One business woman related how a bank manager directed all his comments about her business to her husband!

Some women do persevere and succeed. Anita Roddick started off with a loan from the bank for her first shop. She founded, and is now the managing director of, The Body Shop International – a cosmetics manufacturer and retailer, operating a world-wide organization marketing natural body-care products. In 1984 she won the Business Woman of the Year Award; and in 1987 The Body Shop was named 'Company of the Year' by the CBI Business Enterprise Award.

After eleven years in business Anita Roddick has broken into the highly competitive international cosmetics market and created nearly 3,000 new jobs. Around 98 per cent of her products were made in Britain, with a quarter of them for export. Anita Roddick shows entrepreneurial flair and a keen business sense, as well as setting an example to other companies by being involved with environmental and community projects, conservation and recycling schemes.

Role models like these are very important, but more facilities for training women which emphasize confidence building and

6
The Department of Employment's Research Paper No. 65 suggested that the government:
. . . could require that enterprise training be built into traditionally female educational sectors, such as Art and Design, catering and hairdressing.
9

Left *Anita Roddick, managing director of the highly successful manufacturer and retailer Body Shop International.*

Above *Joanna Foster, chairperson of the Equal Opportunities Commission since May 1988, previously set up the Pepperell Unit for women in industry.*

assertiveness, and a more sensitive approach by those financing small businesses would reduce the stresses that new business women encounter.

Many successful business women act as 'mentors', helping aspiring business women by advising, counselling and sharing experiences with them. Other women stand out in their tireless attempts to improve the opportunities for women in business. One example is Lady Howe, who served as deputy chairperson on the Equal Opportunities Commission from 1974–9.

Lady Elspeth Howe JP (b. 1932)

Lady Howe was born in London in 1932. After leaving school in 1950 she took a secretarial course and, aged twenty, became the secretary to the principal of the Architectural Association's School of Architecture.

She married Geoffrey Howe in August 1953 and gave up her job in 1955 to have her first child. By 1959 she was the wife of a young Member of Parliament and a mother to three young children. She combined this with a wide range of voluntary work in law and education. She became governor of Hay Currie Secondary Modern School, Poplar, in 1958 and has been a magistrate in the Inner London Juvenile Court since 1964.

From 1961–8 she was manager and vice-chairperson of various nursery and primary schools in Tower Hamlets, and throughout the 1960s and 1970s continued to serve as governor of various schools, a remand home and the Froebel Education Institute. Since 1970 she has been chairperson of a London Juvenile Court. In 1978 she was the vice-president of the Pre-School Playgroups Management Committee, working to change attitudes, involve parents, and provide training programmes.

From September 1974 to May 1979 she served as deputy-chairperson of the Equal Opportunities Commission. Her work enabled her to promote equal opportunities for women in employment and education. In 1979 her husband, Sir Geoffrey, became Chancellor of the Exchequer and because of her additional role as the 'treasury spouse' she thought it was in everyone's interests to step down from the EOC.

As a member of the Equal Opportunities Board she frequently urged women to opt

Lady Howe has worked hard to improve equal opportunities.

for further education, and in 1982 Lady Howe herself began a degree course at the London School of Economics in Social Science and Administration. Lady Howe's work in equal opportunities for women, and in law and education continues to flourish. She is currently chairperson of Business in the Community's new Women's Economic Development Initiative and of a Hansard Society commission which is looking at the barriers that prevent women obtaining top jobs. She is also the founder patron of Women into Business. She emphasizes the need for flexibility in employment which would help women with children, and wants to tap the resources of older women, including the over-sixties who have years of experience and expertise to offer.

9

The Way Ahead

A child playing happily at Brighton Borough Council's workplace nursery. British business women will never be able to reach their full potential while Britain has the lowest number of nursery schools in western Europe.

Changing ideas about socially acceptable behaviour for working women and shifts in the economy have directly affected the numbers of women able to participate in the business world. The achievements of business women are especially remarkable throughout the nineteenth and twentieth centuries because they succeeded in a male-dominated economy, and often in the face of adverse public opinion.

In 1931 only one in ten married women worked outside the home. By 1951 one in five went out to work, and by the mid-1970s the figure was one in two. This gradually increasing number of women in paid employment is largely due to changes in domestic commitments. Birth-control and the resulting ability to avoid continuous pregnancy, means that the proportion of women's lives now spent with children at home is decreasing.

The increased number of women available for work is also a result of the extended life expectancy of women and the return of older women to work. Improved education has meant more equal training opportunities. Many more women now have better qualifications and, as a result, are investing more time in their careers, rather than making marriage the sole focus of their lives.

To overcome the problems business women face today requires determination and energy. Business men can expect a great deal of domestic and business support from wives, who provide a variety of hidden and unpaid services to their husband's businesses – from keeping accounts to taking orders on the phone. Potential business women cannot always rely on husbands for the same support, and as a result often carry the full burden of the business and the domestic commitments. To achieve success many women have had to follow male career patterns, which do not allow a career break for child rearing.

In 1992 British women will be able to sell products and services in Europe, which will be a single market the size of Japan and the USA put together. At the moment, Britain is far behind other countries in the provisions it offers to enable business

'*The appeal of business proprietorship will persist because it offers, if only to a variable and limited extent, a measure of autonomy which many women would otherwise be unable to enjoy.*
From *Women in Charge* by R Goffee and R Scase.'

In 1989 the top five winners of the London Livewire award for new businesses, sponsored by National Westminster Bank, were all women. The scheme encourages people under twenty-six to work for themselves in business, co-operative or community projects.

6

The late twenties and early thirties are identified as the crucial period of career life . . . These are the precise years in which, for many women, family commitments are likely to be at their most demanding. From *In a Man's World* edited by Anne Spencer and David Podmore.

9

women to contribute to the economy. To date Britain has the lowest number of nursery schools in Western Europe, and those which do exist only look after children for half a day, meaning mothers are only available for part-time work.

However, the early 1990s will see a drop in the number of school-leavers, and therefore greater competition among companies to attract graduates and to keep staff, particularly women. The government and many companies will find they have to change their child-care policies to draw mothers back to work. As they have been throughout history, market forces in the last years of the twentieth century will probably be a determining factor in bringing about a change in attitude to business women.

A variety of forces – economic, social and political – will shape the development of women's businesses in the 1990s. Over the last twenty years the Women's Liberation Movement has opened many women's eyes to the inequalities women face, and it will continue to improve the chances of women's success in what is still a man's world.

Projects

See how much evidence you can collect about the activities of business women. You could concentrate on past business women, or on those women working in business today. If you decide to collect information about past business women, look for evidence in your local library, museum and art gallery. Old newspapers and church archives can be useful sources. Try visiting your local Public Record Office for information on what kind of businesses women have worked in. A book that might help you organize your project is *Discovering Women's History: a practical manual* by Deirdre Beddoe (Pandora Press, 1983).

To collect information on present-day business women look for information in newspapers, magazines and on television. What sorts of businesses are women involved in? Try to compare how much time and space are given to business women and to business men.

Do you know any women who own their own businesses? Ask if you can interview them. Try to find out exactly what they do, and how they got started in business. Ask what kind of difficulties they faced at first, and how they got round them. Try to categorize the women according to how they balance their business commitments with their domestic lives. For example, do they have children? Do they work from home? What are their reasons for running the business?

Some useful addresses to help with your research are:

The Fawcett Library (a women's history and women's studies library), City of London Polytechnic, Calcutta House, Old Castle Street, London E1 7NT.

The Pepperell Unit Robert Hyde House, 48 Bryanston Square, London W1H 7LN.

Women into Business Suite 46, Westminster Palace Gardens, Artillery Row, London SW1P 1RR.

The Industrial Society 3 Carlton House Terrace, London SW1Y 5DG.

The Equal Opportunities Commission Overseas House, Quay Street, Manchester M3 3HN.

Women's Enterprise Development Agency Aston Science Park, Lovel Lane, Aston Triangle, Birmingham B7 4BJ.

Books to Read

Books for younger readers

Beddoe, Deirdre *Discovering Women's Rights: a practical manual* (Pandora Press, 1983)

Einhorn, Barbara *Let's Discuss Women's Rights* (Wayland, 1988)

Macdonald, Fiona *Working for Equality* (Virago, 1987)

Books for older readers

Clutterbuck, David & Devine, Marion (eds.) *Businesswoman: Present and Future* (Macmillan, 1987)

Corina, Maurice *Pile it High and Sell it Cheap* (Weidenfeld & Nicolson, 1971)

Davidoff, Leonore & Westover, Belinda (eds.) *Our Work, Our Lives, Our Words* (Macmillan Educational, 1986)

Fowler, Deborah *The Woman's Guide to Starting Your Own Business* (Thorsons, 1984)

Goffee, Robert & Scase, Richard *Women in Charge: The Experiences of Female Entrepreneurs* (Allen & Unwin, 1985)

Groocock, Veronica *Women Mean Business* (Ebury Press, 1988)

Hertz, Leah *The Business Amazons* (Methuen, 1987)

Holdsworth, Angela *Out of the Doll's House* (BBC Publications, 1988)

Pinchbeck, Ivy *Women Workers and the Industrial Revolution* (George Routledge & Sons, 1930)

Taylor Bradford, Barbara *A Woman of Substance* (Granada Publishing, 1981)

Vicinus, Martha (ed.) *A Widening Sphere – Changing Roles of Victorian Women* (Methuen, 1980)

Whitelegg, E & Arnot, M (eds.) *The Changing Experience of Women* (Open University Press, 1982)

Women Directors – Who's Who in the World of Women Directors (Eurofi UK, 1987)

Glossary

amalgamation The process of combining or uniting.

analyst A person who examines something in detail to discover meaning.

annuity A sum paid at fixed intervals (often annually) over a specific period of time, such as the recipient's life.

apprentice Someone who works for a skilled person, for a fixed period of time, in order to learn a trade.

assets Any property, stock or money owned by a person or business, which can be used to pay or guarantee debts.

benefactress A woman who helps a person or institution, especially by giving money.

broker An agent who, acting on another person's behalf, buys and sells goods for a commission.

cabinet The group of leading, policy-making government ministers.

capital The lump sum of money, or stock with which a person enters into business.

commerce Activities to do with buying and selling goods and services.

consolidate To make something whole, or to make something stronger and more stable.

co-operative A business or enterprise owned by its workers, and run for joint economic benefit.

crèche A day nursery for very young children.

directory A book listing the names and addresses of individuals or firms.

economic recession A period of economic hardship.

economics The study and analysis of people's production and use of goods and services.

economy The management of money and materials.

enterprise A bold, difficult undertaking; a business or company.

entrepreneur A person who sets up a business enterprise, with the chance of profit or loss.

executive Someone responsible for managing part, or all, of a project or business.

feminist A supporter of equal rights for women.

institution An organization founded for a worthwhile cause, such as a hospital or college.

liquid property Property that can easily be changed into money.

lucrative Profitable.

marriage bar The law that prevented women from working after marriage.

moral The distinction between good and bad, right and wrong human behaviour.

morality A system of morals.

premises The land and buildings in which a business is situated.

public relations The practice of creating and promoting a good impression of a business.

radical A person who favours extreme change.

retailer Someone involved in selling goods individually, or in small quantities direct to consumers.

session papers Records of court meetings in which business has been transacted.

stereotype A standardized, conventional image of a type of person shared by many people.

Stock Exchange The highly organized market in the City of London where company shares are bought and sold.

transactions Business deals and negotiations.

transition The change from one state or stage to another.

trustee A person who is entrusted to look after a business or property on behalf of someone else.

whey The watery liquid that separates from the solid curd when milk is clotted.

wholesaler Someone who sells goods in large quantities to the shopkeeper rather than directly to the public.

Index

Numbers in **bold** indicate illustrations.

Anderson, Adelaide 18
apprentices 4, 7, 17
Ashley, Laura 38
awards **4**, 38, **44**

banking 20, 22, 27, 29
Barnes, Mair **40**, 40
birth-control 43
Body Shop International 40
bookselling 5, 6
Boucherett, Jessie 16
brokers 22
'business girls' 4
Business Woman of the Year Award **4**, 38–9, **40**, 40

capital 7, 9, 10, 23, 38
career prospects 18, 21
charity work **13**, 14–15
child-birth 9, 33, 43
child care 31, **33**, 33, **43**, 44
Church **10**, 11
Civil Service 17, 18, 24
clerical workers 4, 17, **20**, 20
coaching companies 5, 12
Cohen, Jack 22, 25
computer industry 31
Confederation of British Industry (CBI) 38
   Business Enterprise Award 40
Covent Garden Market 4

dairying **5**, 12
Denmark
   child care in 33
department stores **16**, 16, **17, 23**
directors, women **31**, 35

economic change 8, 31
education 19, 44
Elementary Education Act (1870) 16
Enterprise Allowance Scheme **37**, 38
entrepreneurs 4, 11, 22, 33, 38
equal opportunities 29, 44
Equal Opportunities Commission 41, 42
Equal Pay Act (1970) 30, 31
Europe 44

factory inspectors 18, **19**
factory workers 15
FI Group 34, 36

financial backing 38, 40
First World War 21
Foster, Joanna **41**

'glass ceiling' 32

Haig Thomas, Margaret 21
hairdressers 7
Harrods 23
Hertz, Leah **39**
home and business **8**, 8, 9, 10
Howe, Lady Elspeth 41, **42**, 42
Hyams, Daisy 22, **25**, 25

Industrial Revolution 8, 10, **12**,12, 13–14
Industrial Society 28, 30, 36
innkeepers **8**, **11**, 11, 12
investments 10

lace-making **15**, 15
loans 40
London Chamber of Commerce 22
London Livewire award **44**
low expectations 32

managers, women, 23
marriage
   as a business transaction **9**, 9
   women's legal position 5–6
marriage bar 19, 21, 24
Married Women's Property Act (1882) 19
mentors 41
merchants 5
middle class
   and business 8, 17
   values of 11
millinery 7, 9
Mirman, Sophie 39
Moore, Debbie 39
morality **10**, 11, 15

needlework 15
networks **37**, 37, 38
nursery schools 44

Pepperell, Elizabeth 28, **30**, 30
Pepperell Unit 30
Pineapple Studios 39
Post Office 17, **18**, 19
   Maria Constance Smith 17–18

promotion 32, 35
property
   ownership of 6, 19
prostitution **14**, 14

qualifications 35
Quant, Mary **26**

retailing
   department stores **16**, 16, **17, 23**, 23
   mass-production 16
Rivers-Bulkeley, Elizabeth 28
Roddick, Anita 38, 40, **41**
role models 38, 40

schools 16
Second World War **24**, 24
Sex Discrimination Act (1975) 30, 31
Sex Disqualification (Removal) Act (1919) 22
sexual discrimination 22, 23, **27**, 27, 32, 38
shareholders 28
Shirley, Steve 34, **36**, 36
shop assistants 16
shopkeepers **6**, **7**, 7
Small Business Bureau 38
Sock Shop International 40
Stock Exchange 4, 28, **29**
Stock Market guides **28**
street traders **5**, 7

technology 31
Tesco 22, **25**, 25
training 16–17, 28–9, 34, 41
typewriters **20**, 20

unemployment 31

Veuve Clicquot Business Woman of the Year Award 4, 38–9, **40**, 40
voting rights 22

wages 18, 20–1, **34**
widows 5, 6, 10
Women into Business **37**, 38, 42
Women's Liberation Movement **26**, 26, **27**, 43
Woolworths 40
work practices 34, 36
workplace nurseries **43**

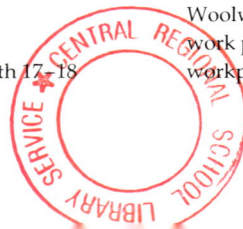